Cute Puppies
A Grayscale Coloring Book for Adults

Dar Payment

The Amazing Grayscale Coloring Company
Lake Elsinore, CA USA

Book design and cover art
By Dar Payment

Photographs sourced from Pixabay and PublicDomainPictures.net

Copyright © 2017 by Dar Payment

All rights reserved. No part of this book may be reproduced, stored in a retrieval system or transmitted, in any form or by any means, electronic, mechanical, photocopying, recording or otherwise, without the prior written consent from the author.

ISBN-13: 978-1976424649

Published by:

The Amazing Grayscale Coloring Company
A Division of DAP Publishing
Lake Elsinore, California USA

www.AmazingGrayscale.com

A Note from the Author

It was not my original intention to put together a coloring book. I am not a professional artist, but I love to color grayscale! And to be honest, the grayscale coloring selection I have shared with you in the following pages of this book are from one of my own private collections.

About a year ago I became totally fascinated with every aspect of coloring – especially with projects concerning grayscale. I was so excited that I began to host small coloring parties with my friends, offering many of the grayscale pages appearing in this book for our coloring inspirations.

My friends loved the coloring projects. Soon they were hooked and told me they wanted more similar grayscale pages to color!

These friends would often show their finished coloring projects with their friends, who wanted to color too . . . and well, the rest is joyful providence. The cumulation of the grayscale coloring book you are now holding in your hands.

Have fun bringing the images to life by filling them up with tons of beautiful color. And if you become obsessed with coloring like I did (and still am) and want to spread the love of coloring with your friends too, host your own coloring party using the pages of this book!

Blessings and Happy Coloring,

Dar Payment

"I prefer living in color." ~ David Hockney

How to Color Grayscale

Coloring grayscale is very easy, and there are a few schools of thought out there about how to color a grayscale image or photograph.

The number one thing about coloring grayscale is that the shading is already there for you which means no more trying to figure out where your light source or shadows need to be, etc..

The first grayscale coloring method is to use one color over each area first using very light pressure over the entire area you wish to color. Next, using the same color apply heavier pressure in the darker shaded areas.

Another method is to simply use your darkest colors to color over the areas with the heaviest gray shading. Then your lighter colors over the areas with the lightest gray shading, and finally using your medium colors to blend both the light and dark colors.

The point is that there is no wrong or right way to color grayscale. So have fun experimenting as you unleash your inner colorist, and enjoy watching as your photo or image comes to life before your eyes.

Need samples of coloring inspirations for the images in this book? Download a free full colored template containing all of the coloring inspirations depicted in this book at: https://www.amazinggrayscale.com/Free-Downloads.php

The Best Artist Mediums for This Book

The best artist mediums for this book are colored pencils. You can experiment with gel pens and markers if you'd like, but gel pens and markers will bleed through the page.

If you do choose to use gel pens or markers the best practice is to put a piece of paper underneath your coloring project in order to protect from bleed through onto the coloring page underneath it.

"Buy a pup and your money will buy you unconditional love".

~ Rudyard Kipling

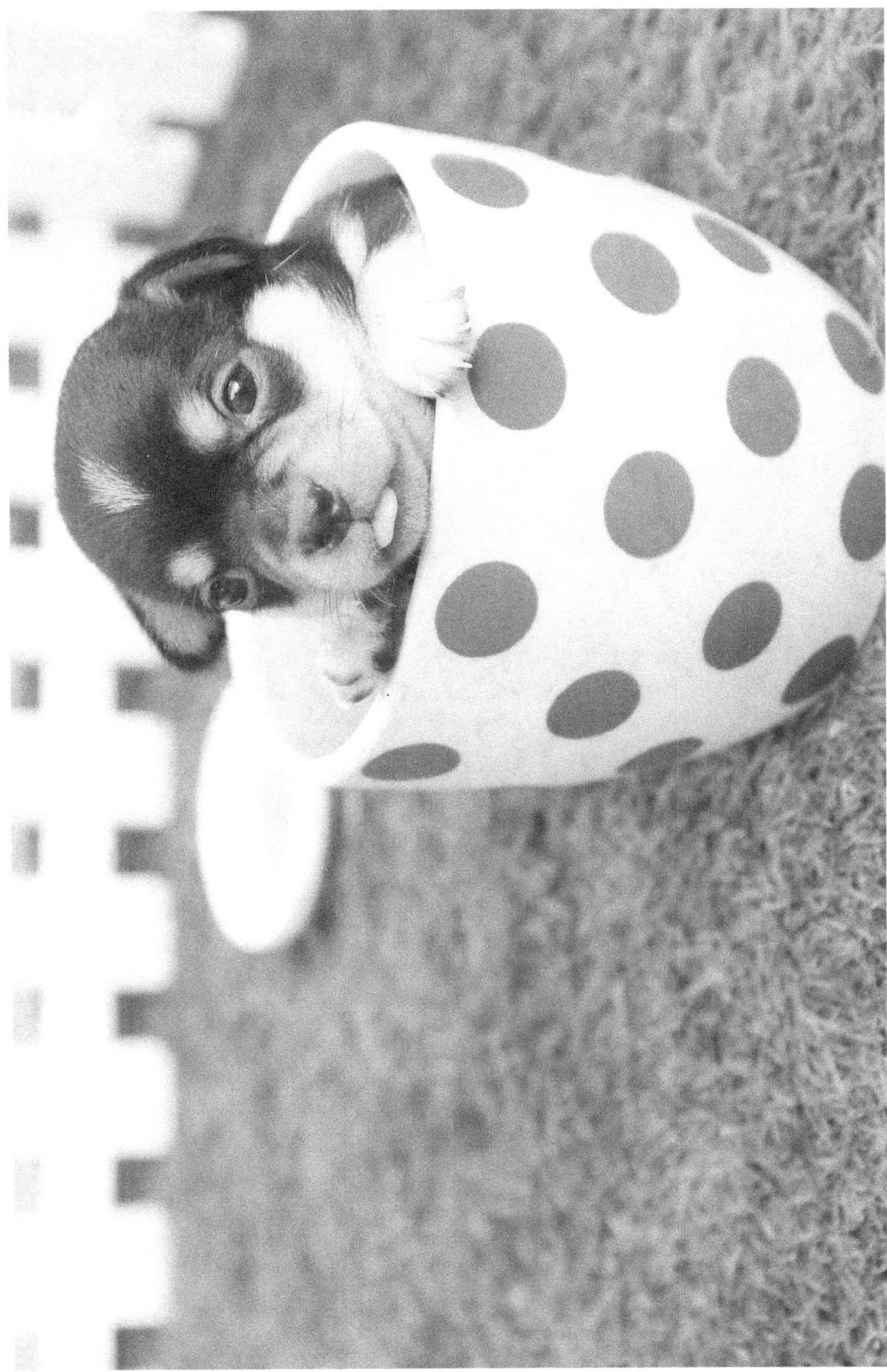

"Puppies are nature's remedy for feeling unloved, plus numerous other ailments of life."
~ Richard Allan Palm

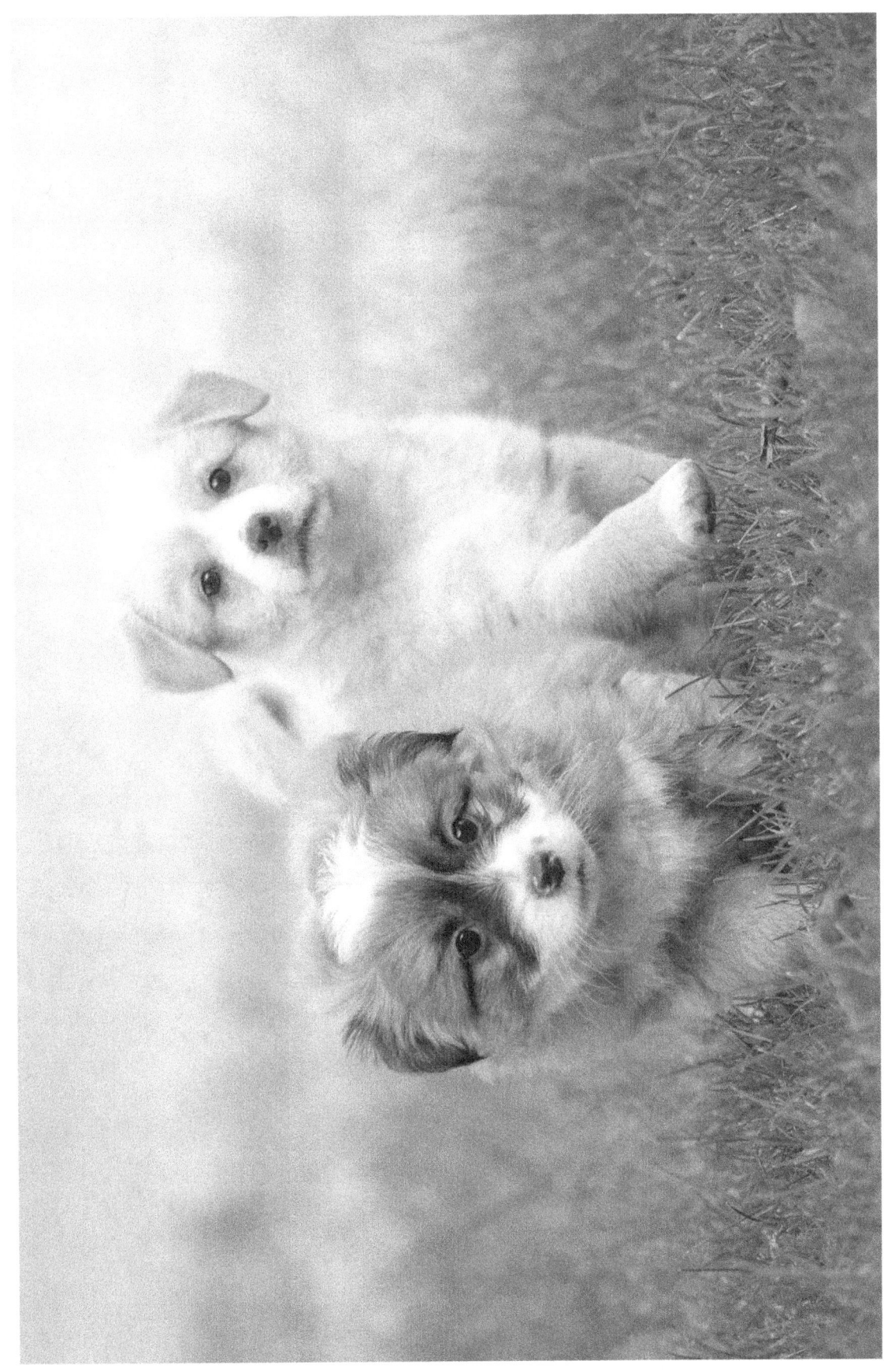

When you feel lousy, puppy therapy is indicated."
~ Sara Paretsky

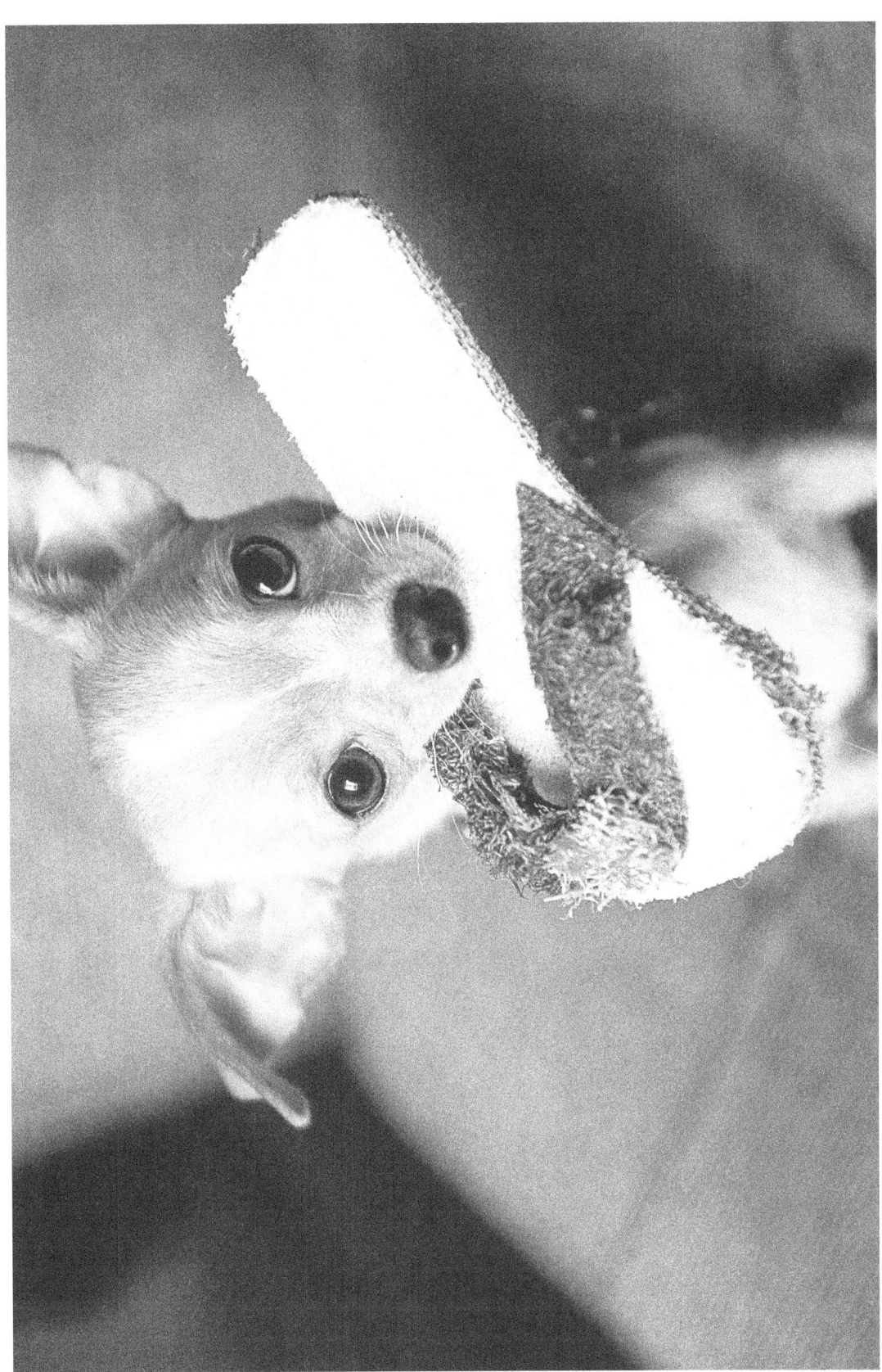

"Of all the things I miss from veterinary practice, puppy breath is one of the most fond memories!"
~ Dr. Tom Cat

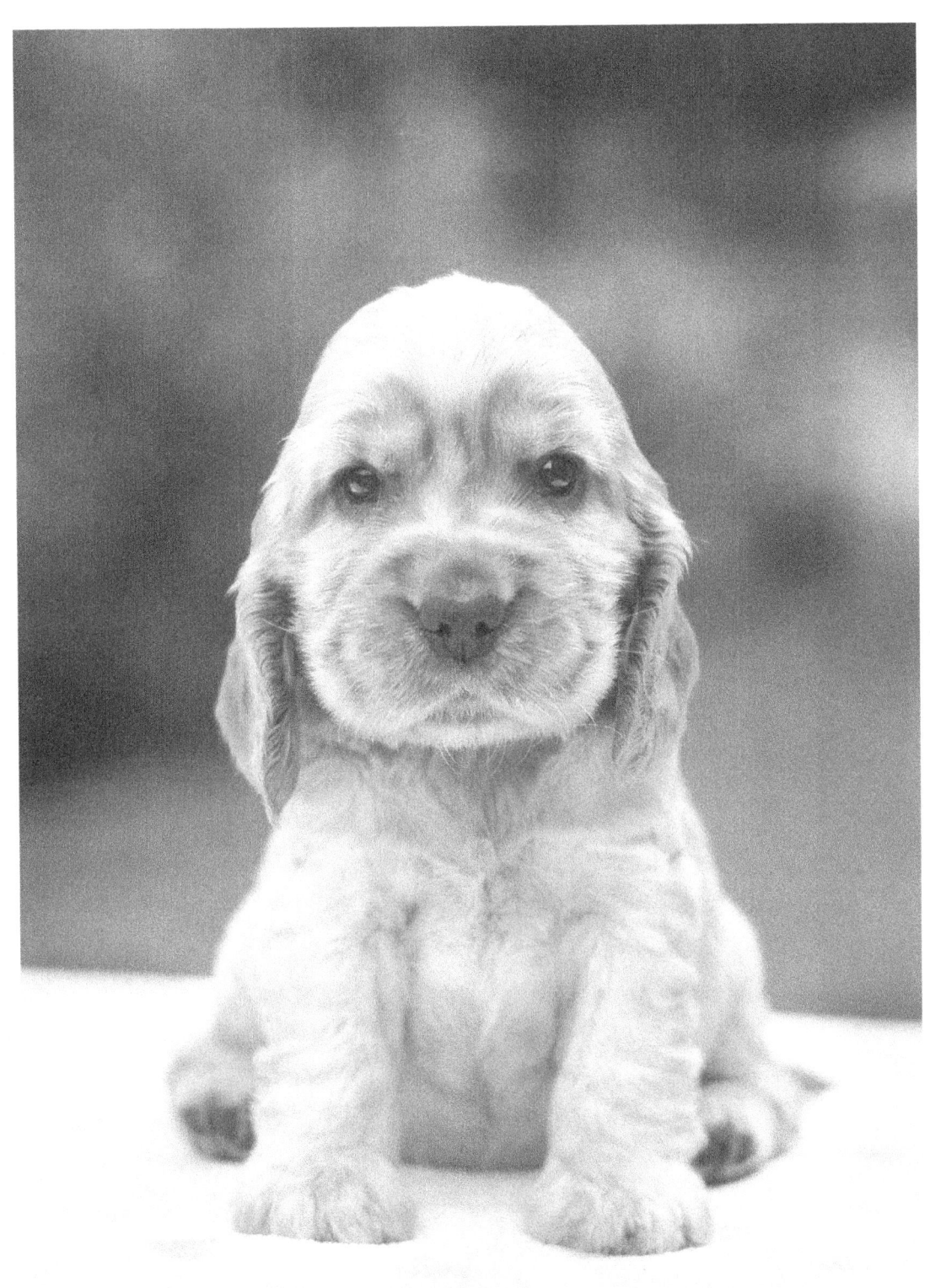

"Every puppy should have a boy. ~ Erma Bombeck

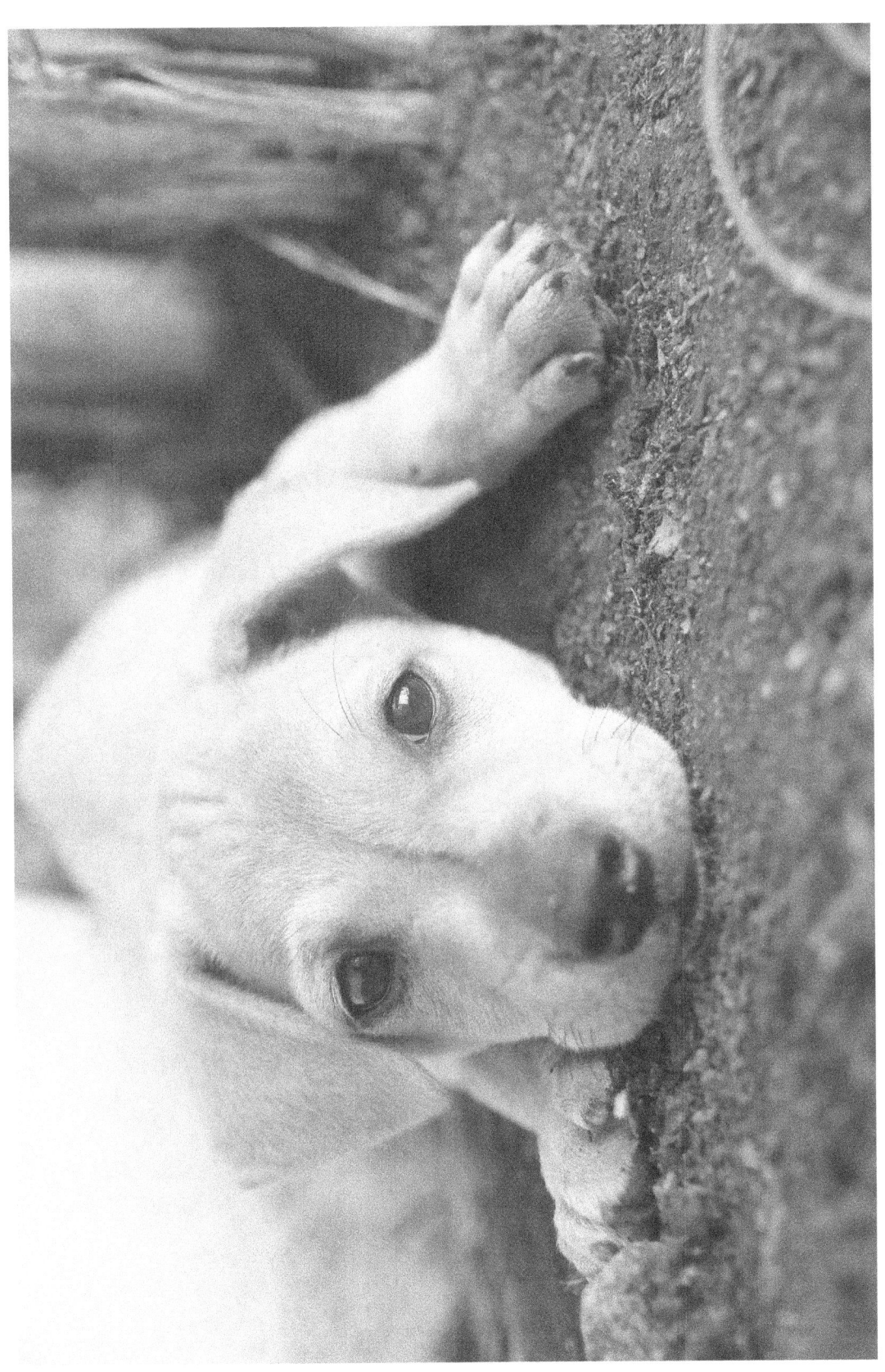

"Whoever said you can't buy happiness
forgot about little puppies."
~ Gene Hill

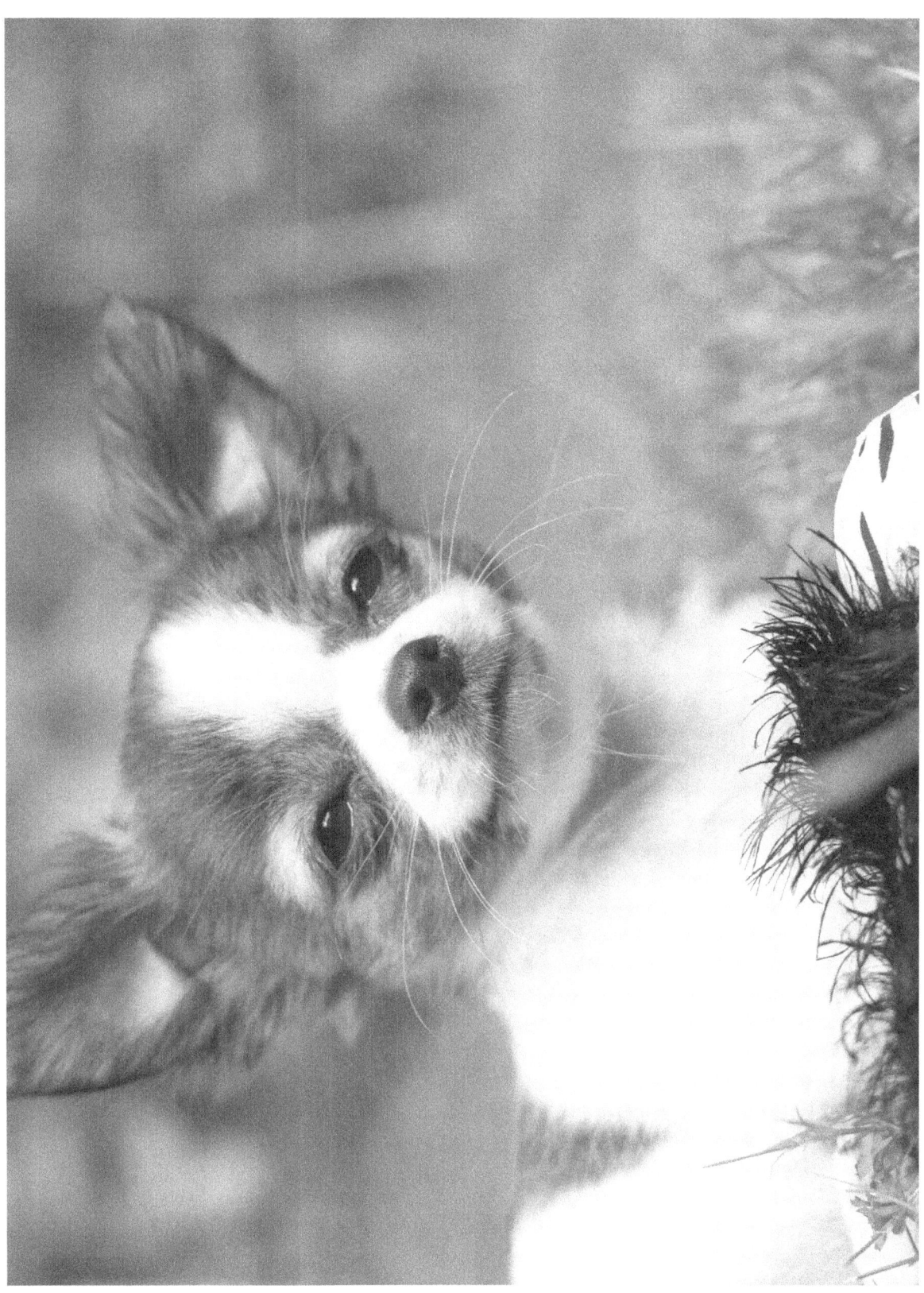

"The best way to get a puppy is to beg for a baby brother—and they'll settle for a puppy every time."
~ Winston Pendleton

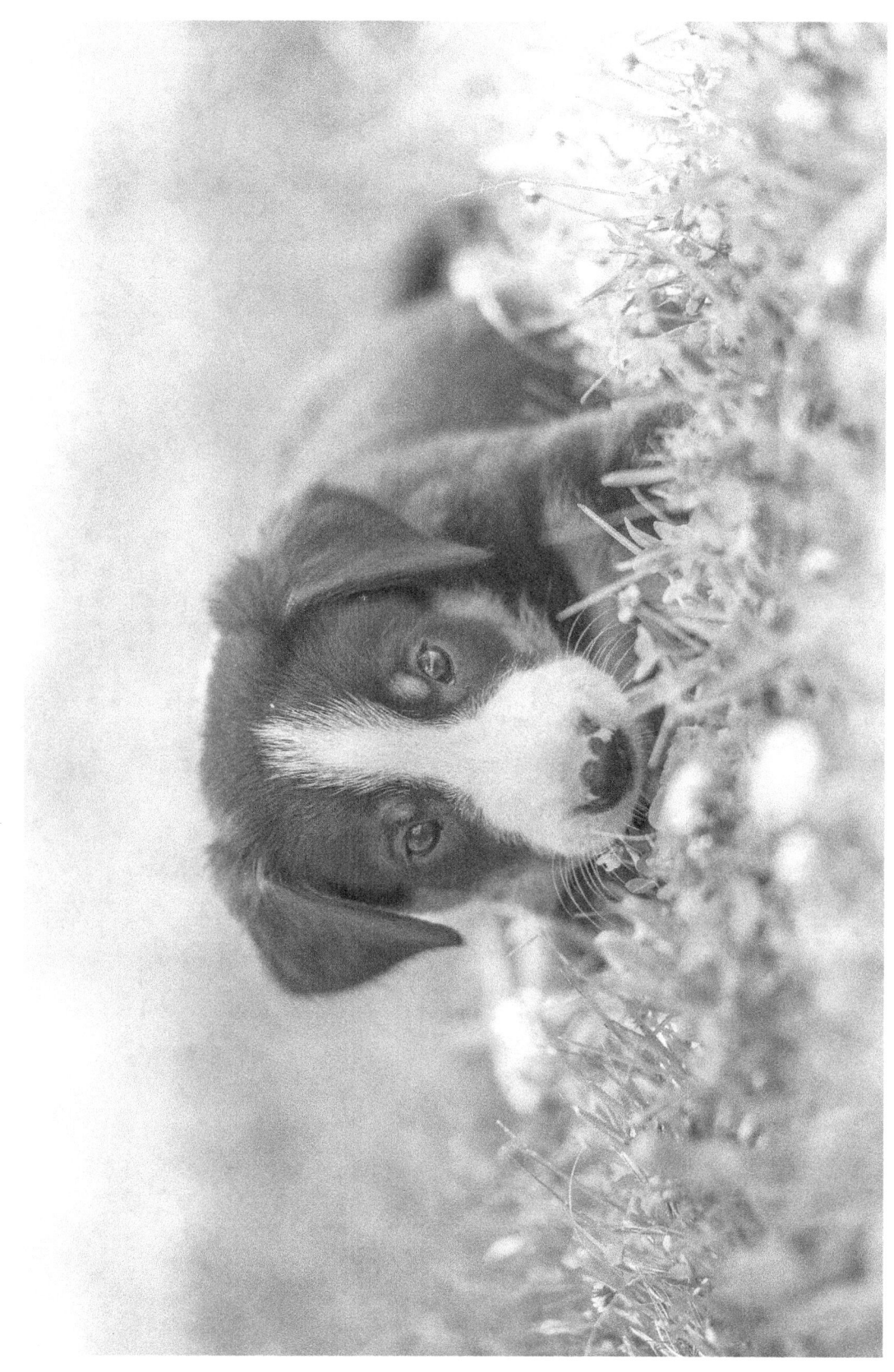

*"There is no psychiatrist in the world
like a puppy licking your face."
~ Bern Williams*

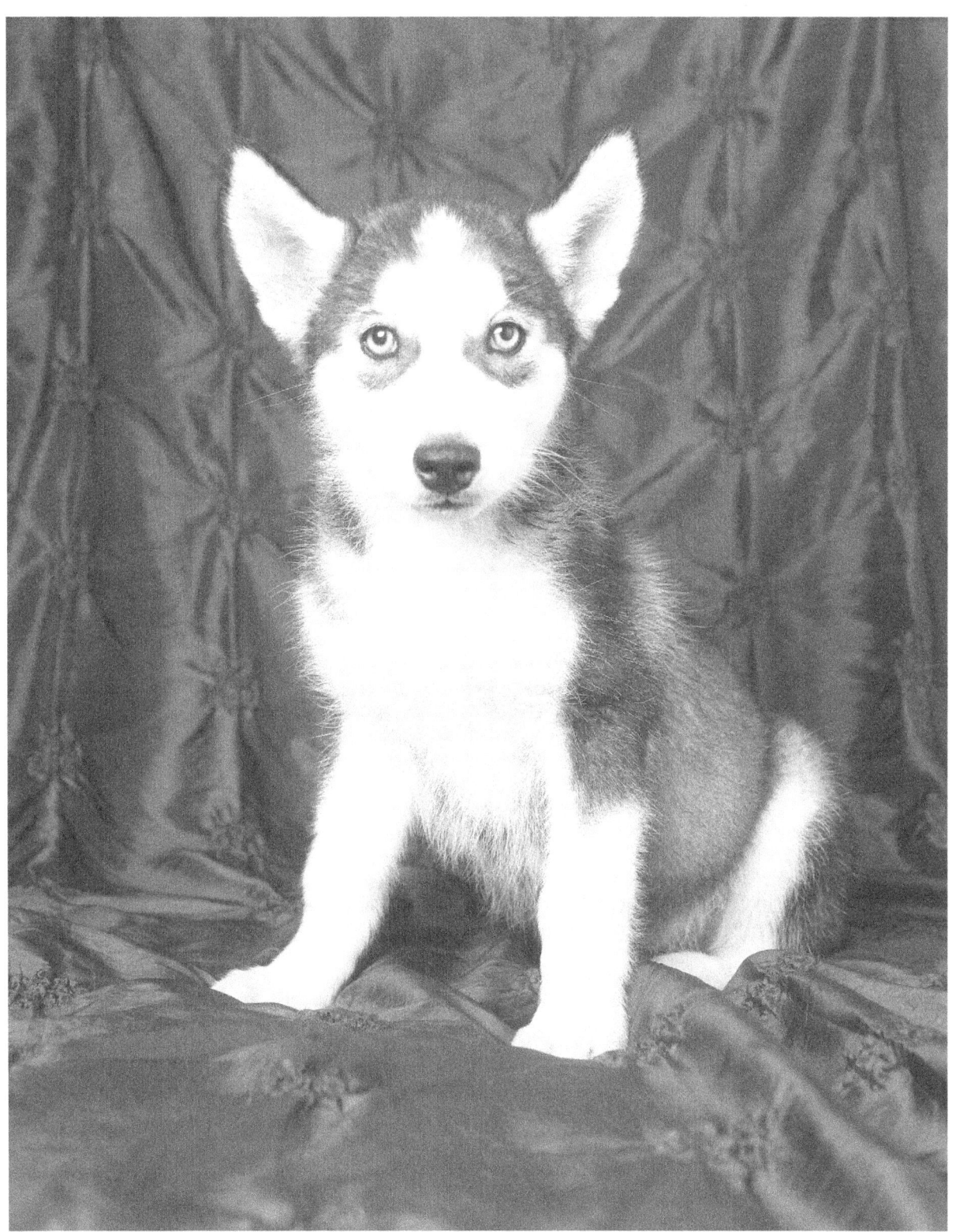

"Happiness is a warm puppy."
~ Charles M. Schulz

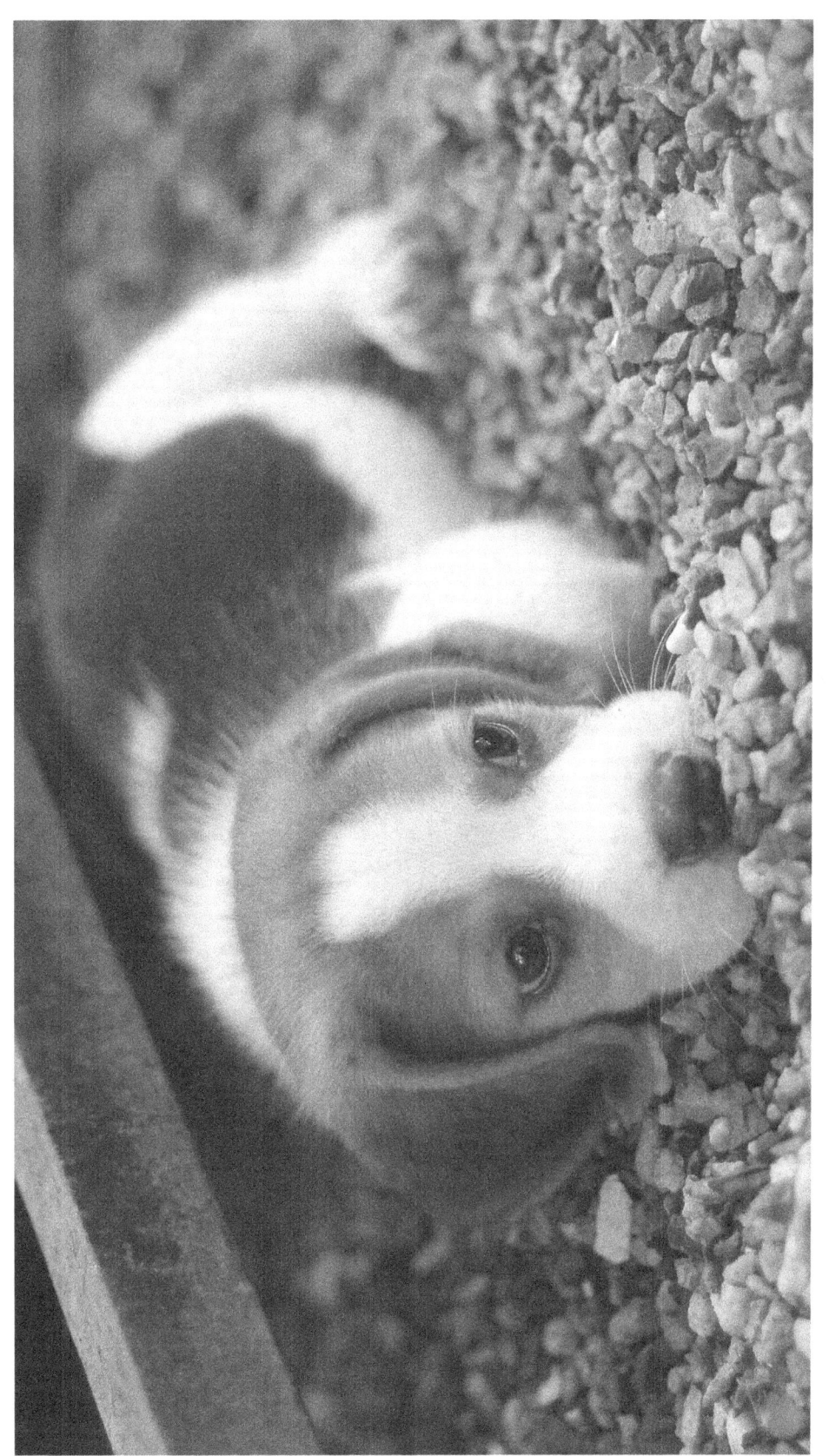

"A dog is the only thing that can mend a crack in your broken heart."
~ Judy Desmond

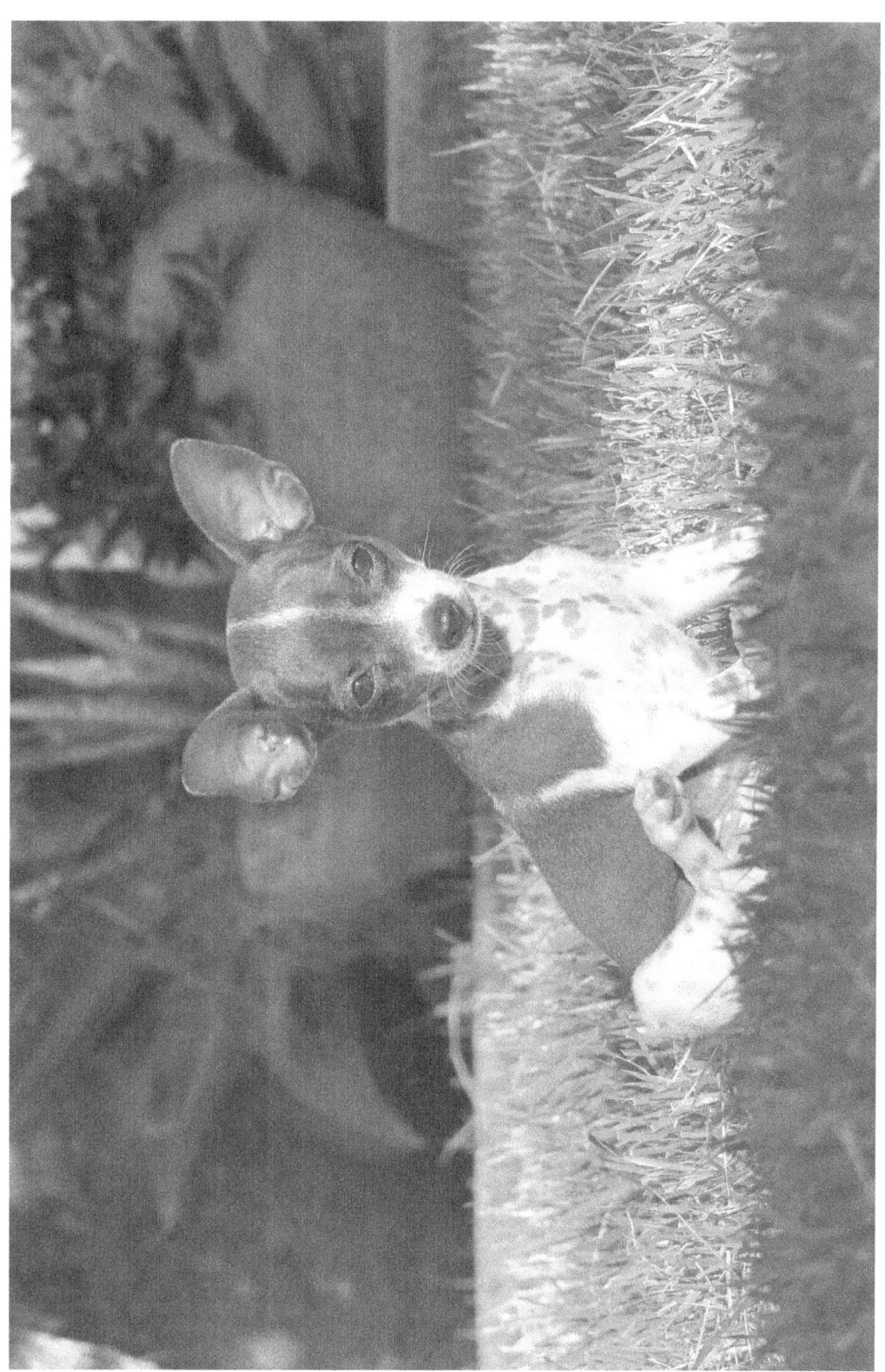

*"Dogs are not our whole life,
but they make our lives whole."
~ Roger Caras*

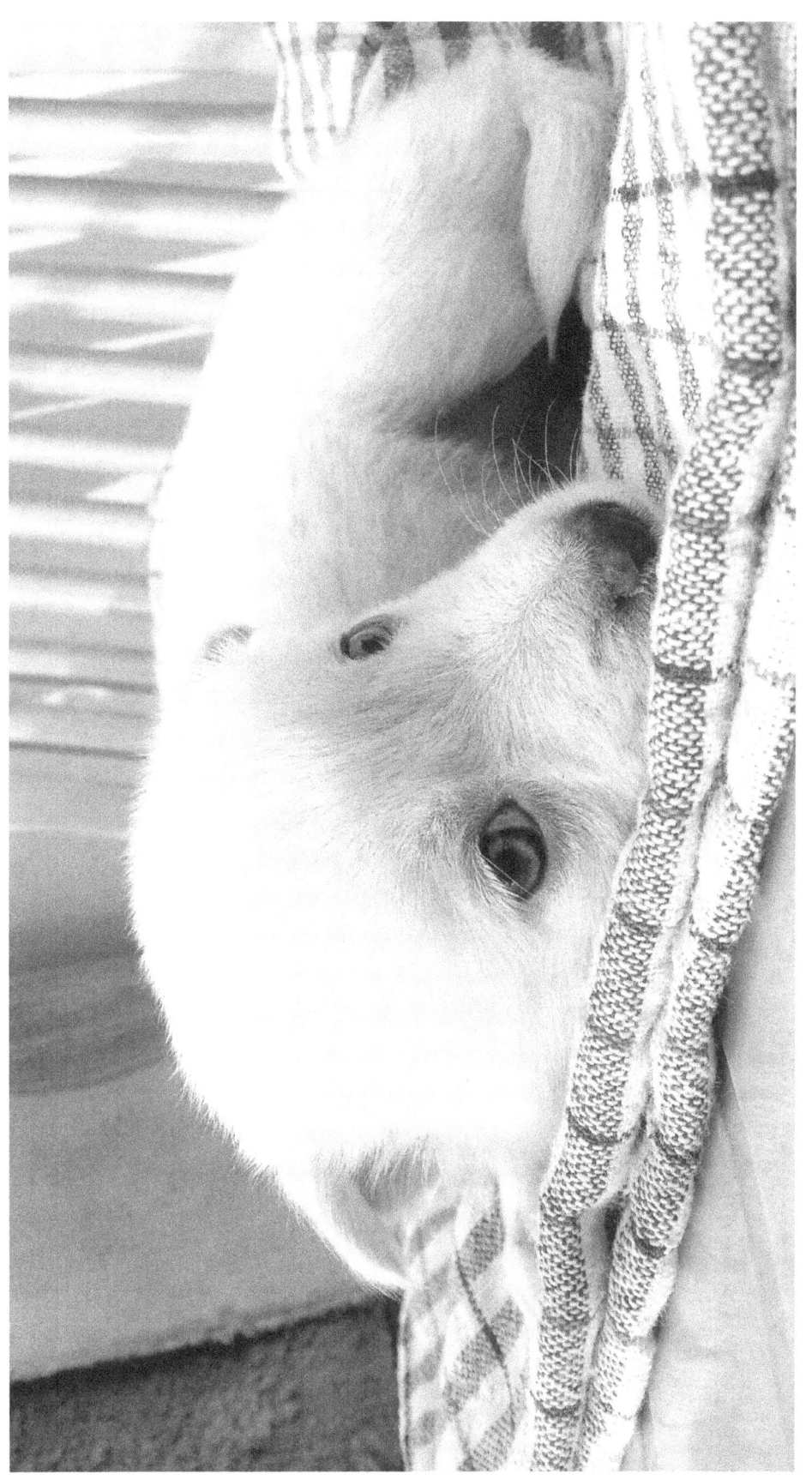

"Dogs act exactly the way we would act if we had no shame."
~ Cynthia Heimel

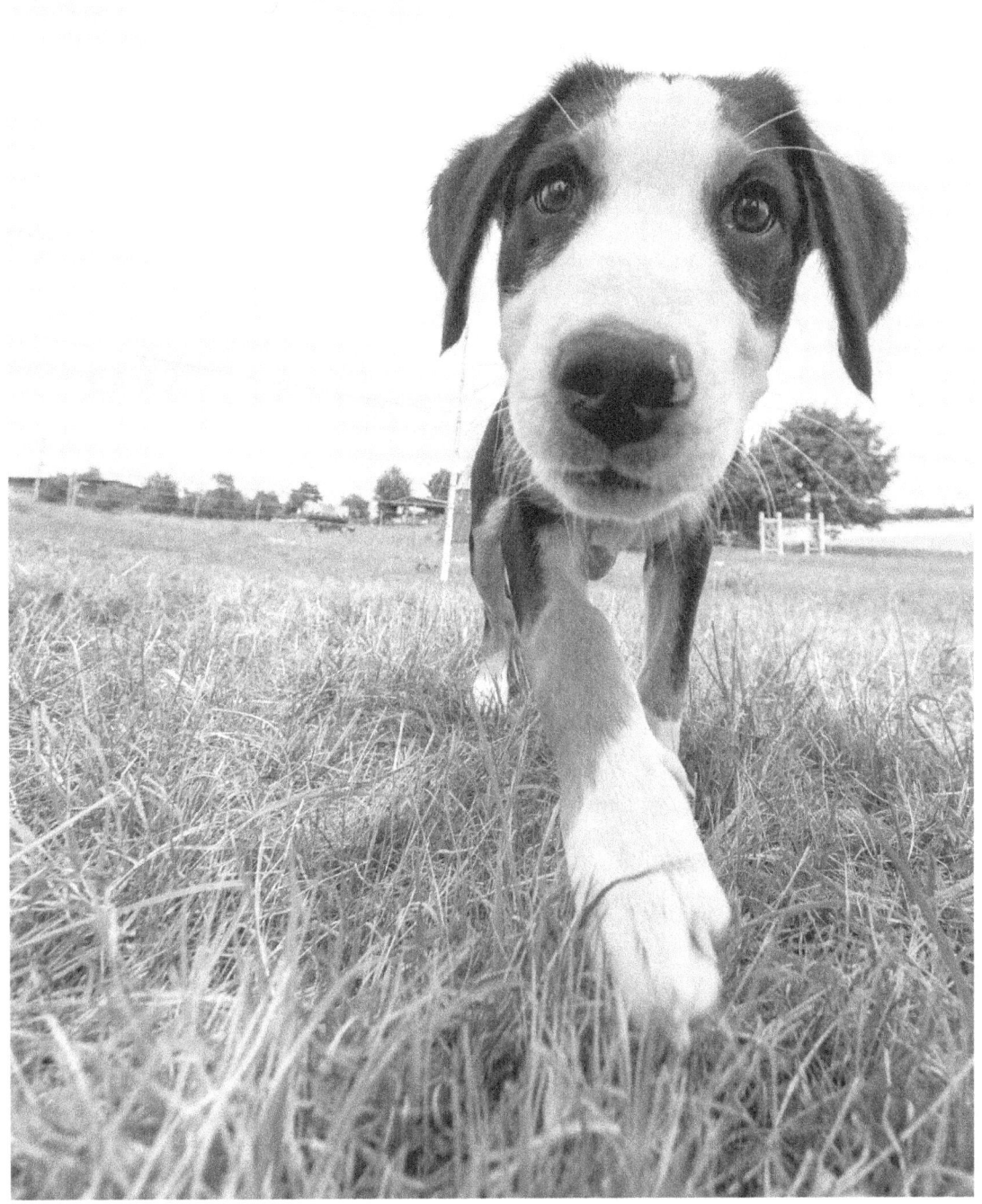

"The only creatures that are evolved enough to convey pure love are puppies and infants."
~ Johnny Depp

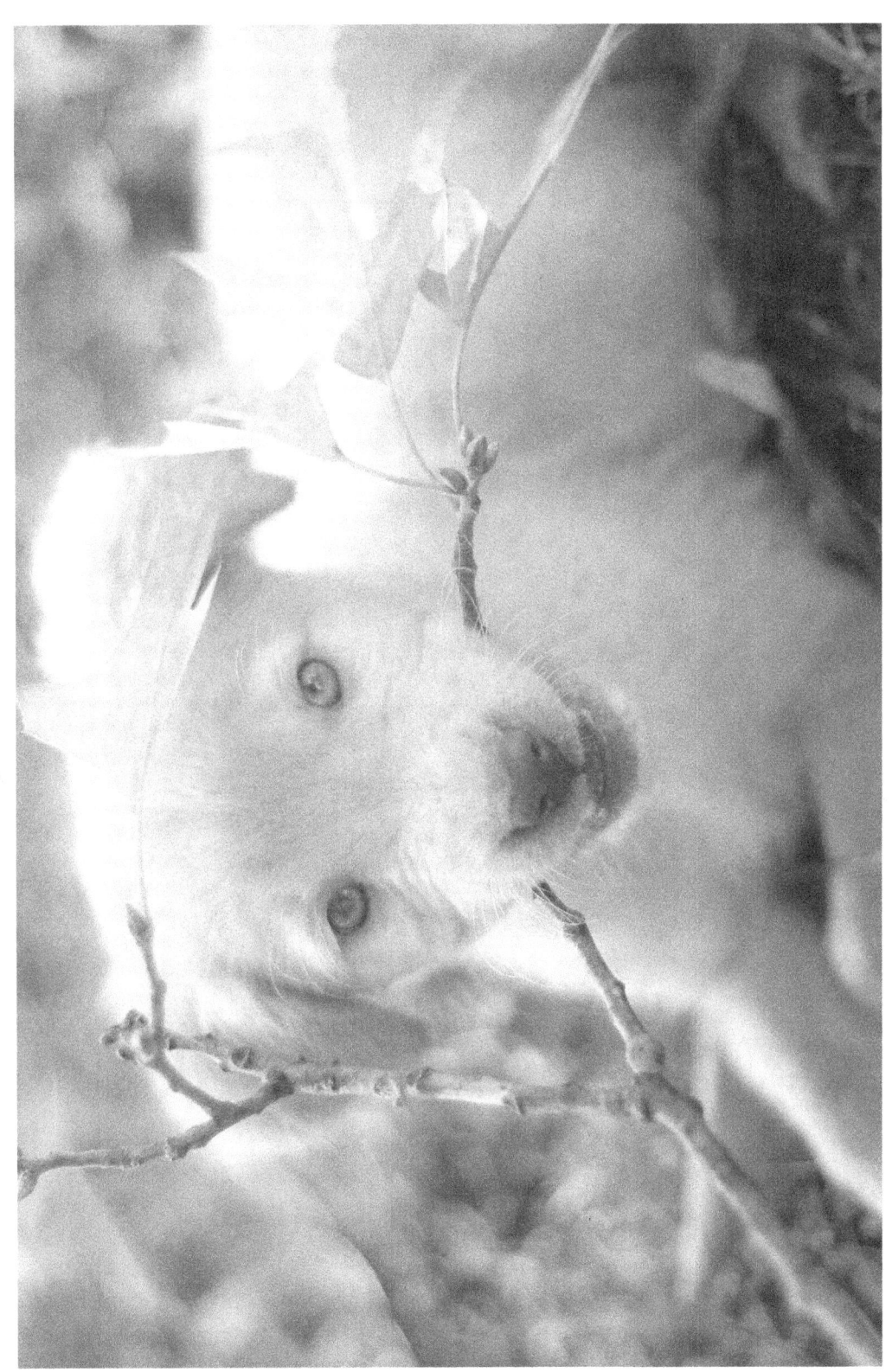

"A dog will teach you unconditional love. If you can have that in your life, things won't be too bad."
~ Robert Wagner

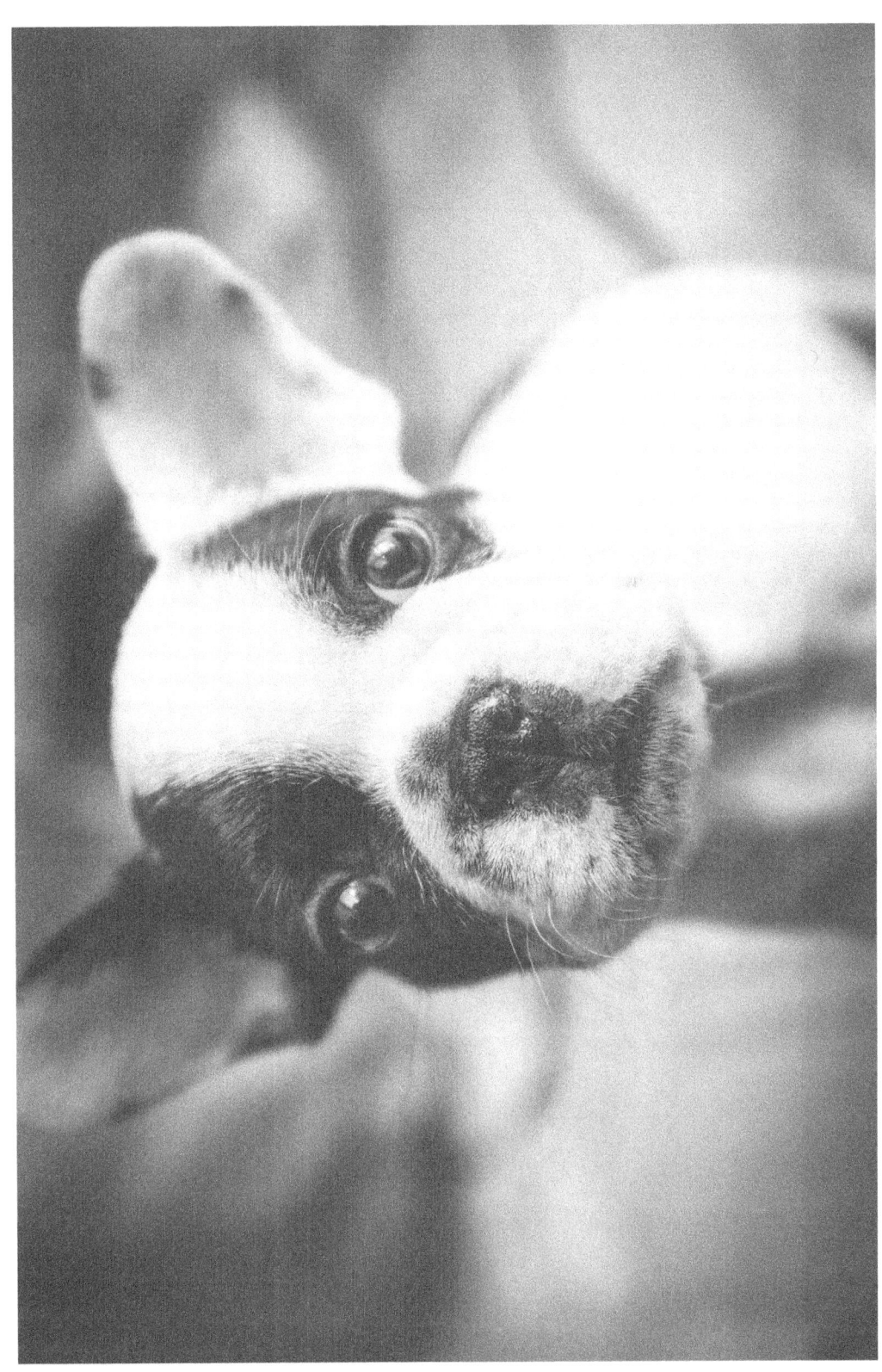

"Puppies not only teach you to be curious, but to also remain present."
~ Anonymous

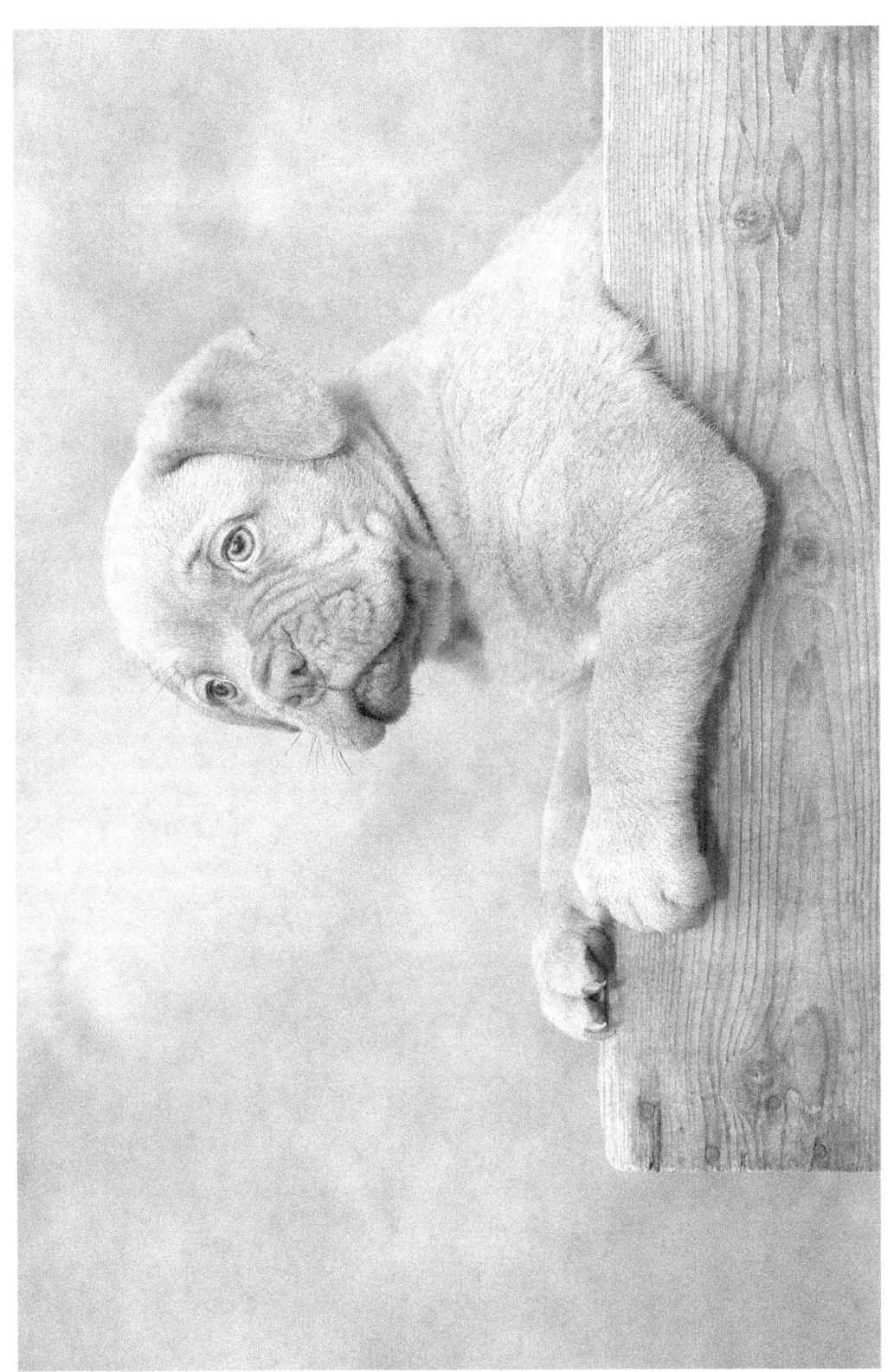

"If you want a wonderful little creature to love you get a puppy."
~ Barbara Walters

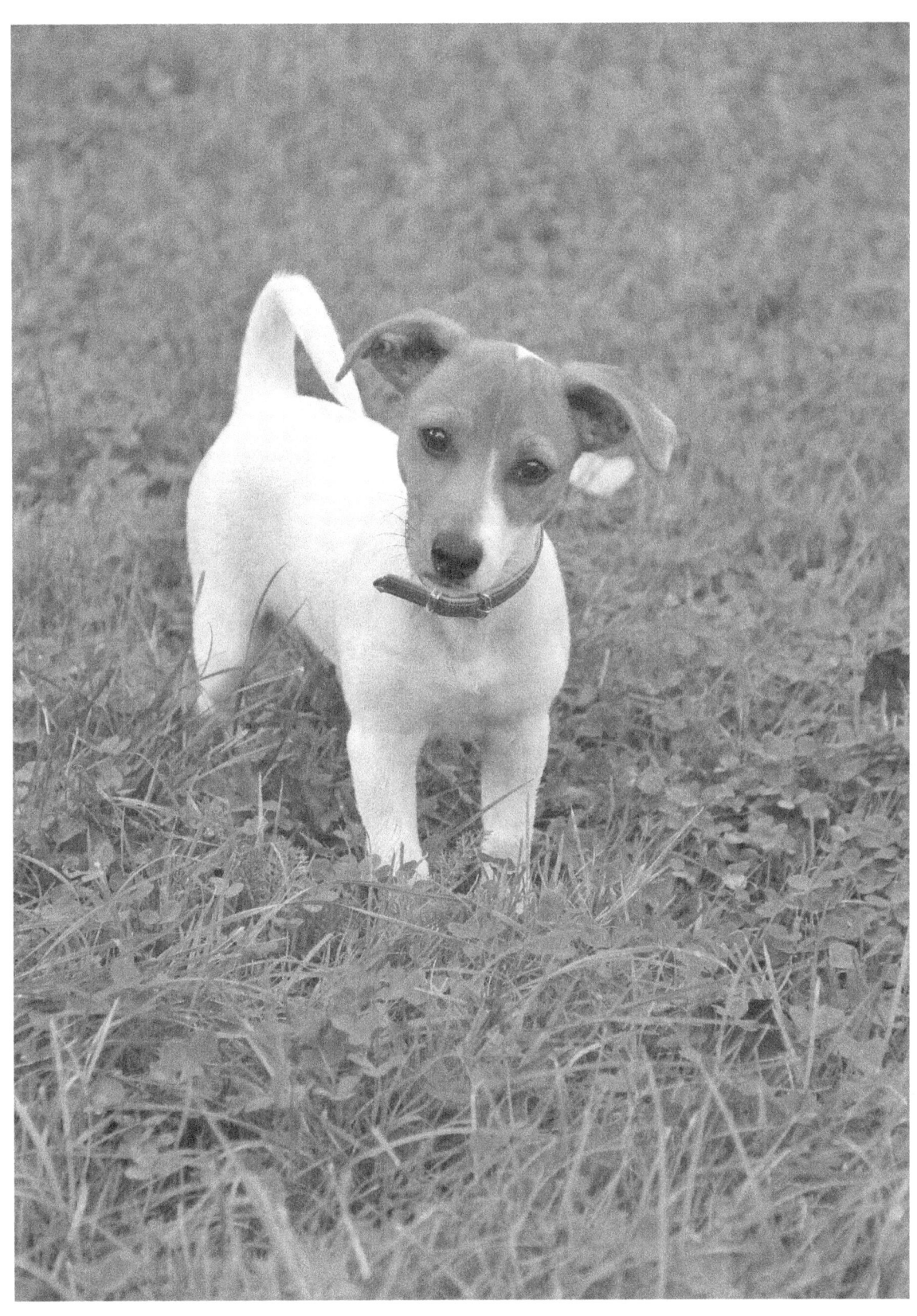

"A puppy is the only thing on earth that loves you more than you love yourself."
~ Josh Billings

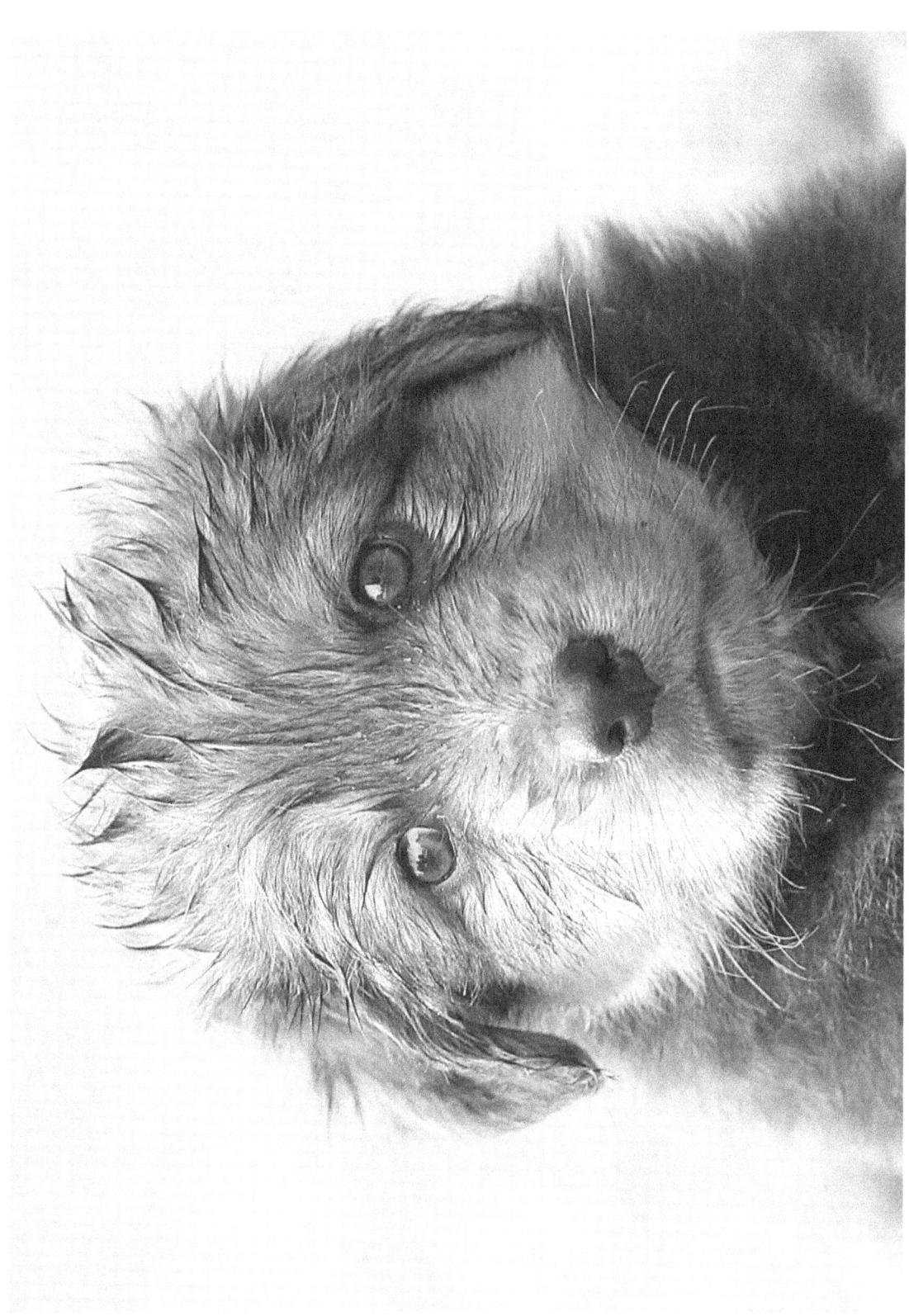

"Scratch a puppy and you have found a permanent job"
~ Franklin P. Jones

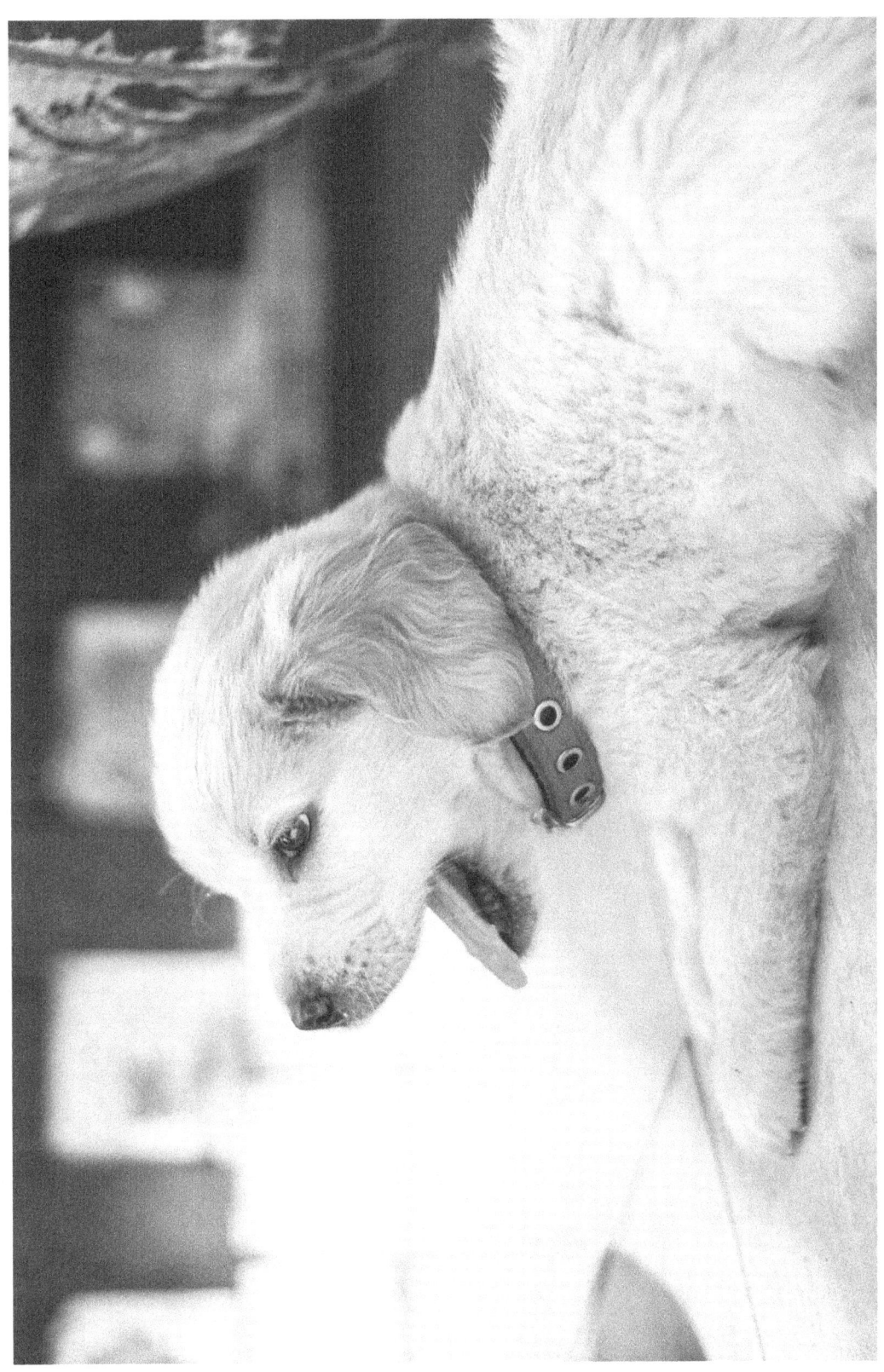

"Did you know that there are over 300 words for love in puppy speak?"
~ Gabriel Zevin

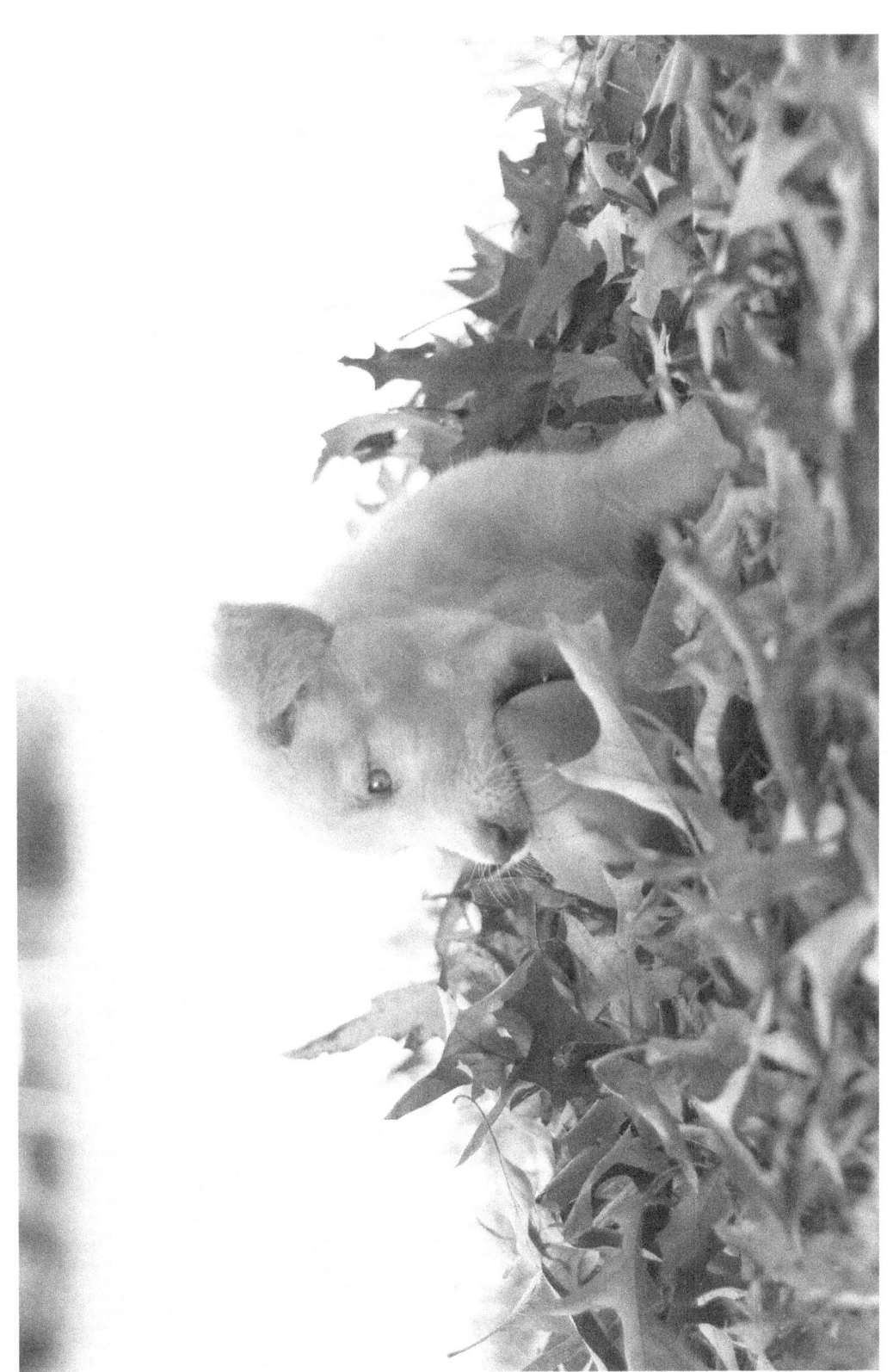

"Ah - the simple life of a pup. Eat, sleep, and play. Wash, rinse, and repeat."
~ Dardarji

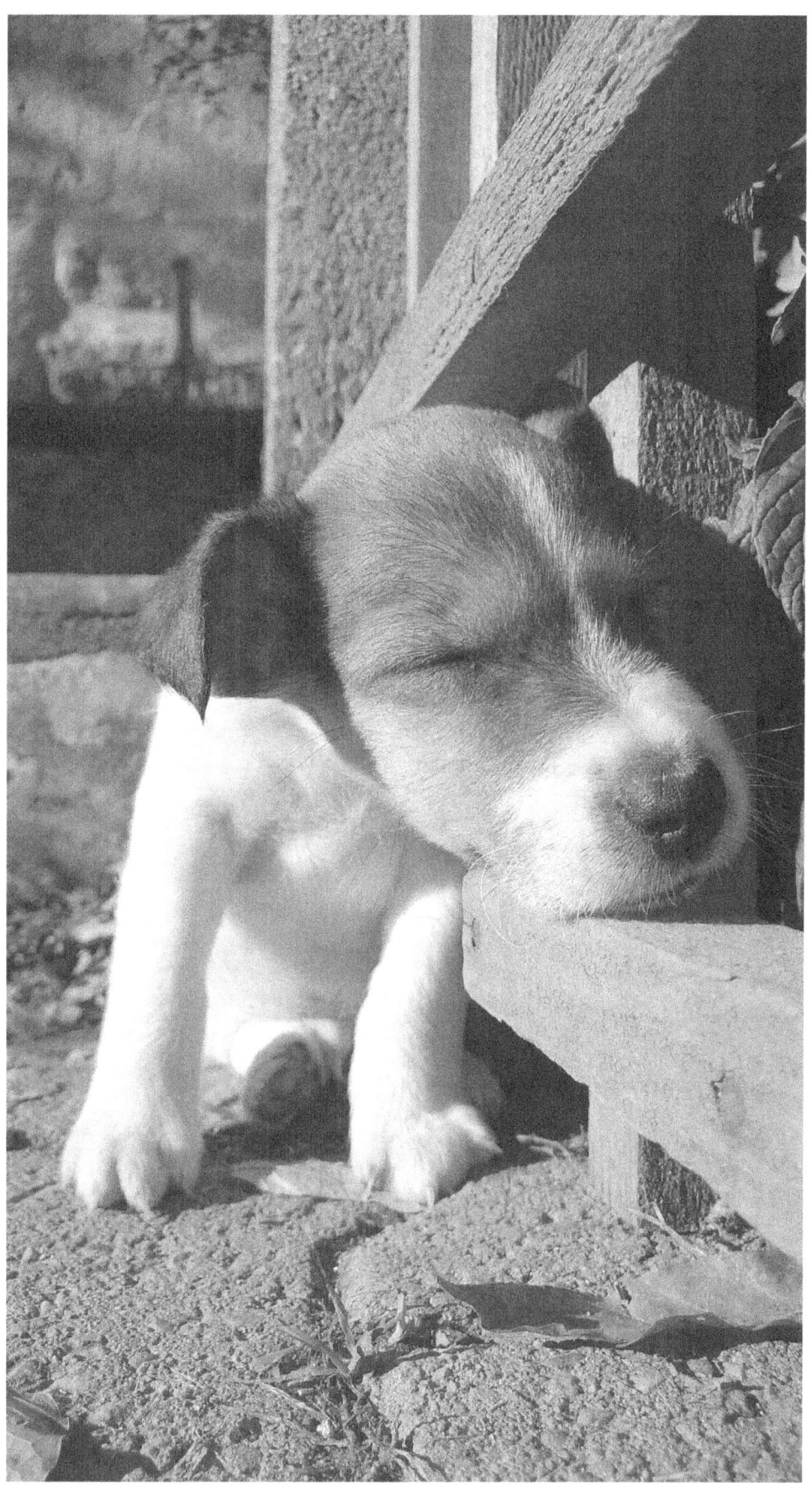

"Puppies are our link to paradise. They don't know evil or jealousy or discontent."
~ Milan Kundera

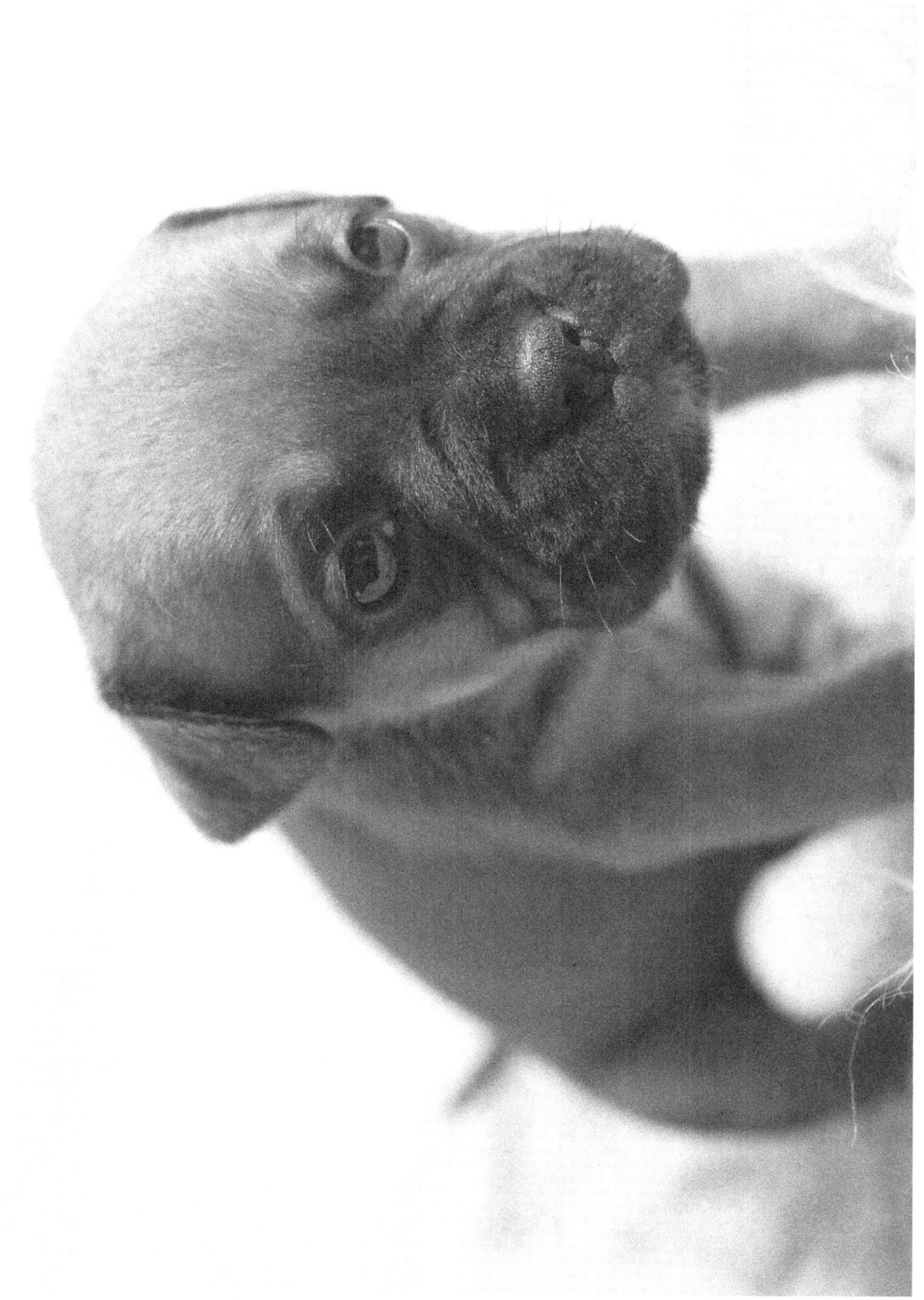

"If a puppy will not come to you after having looked you in the face, you should go home and examine your conscience.""
~ Woodrow Wilson

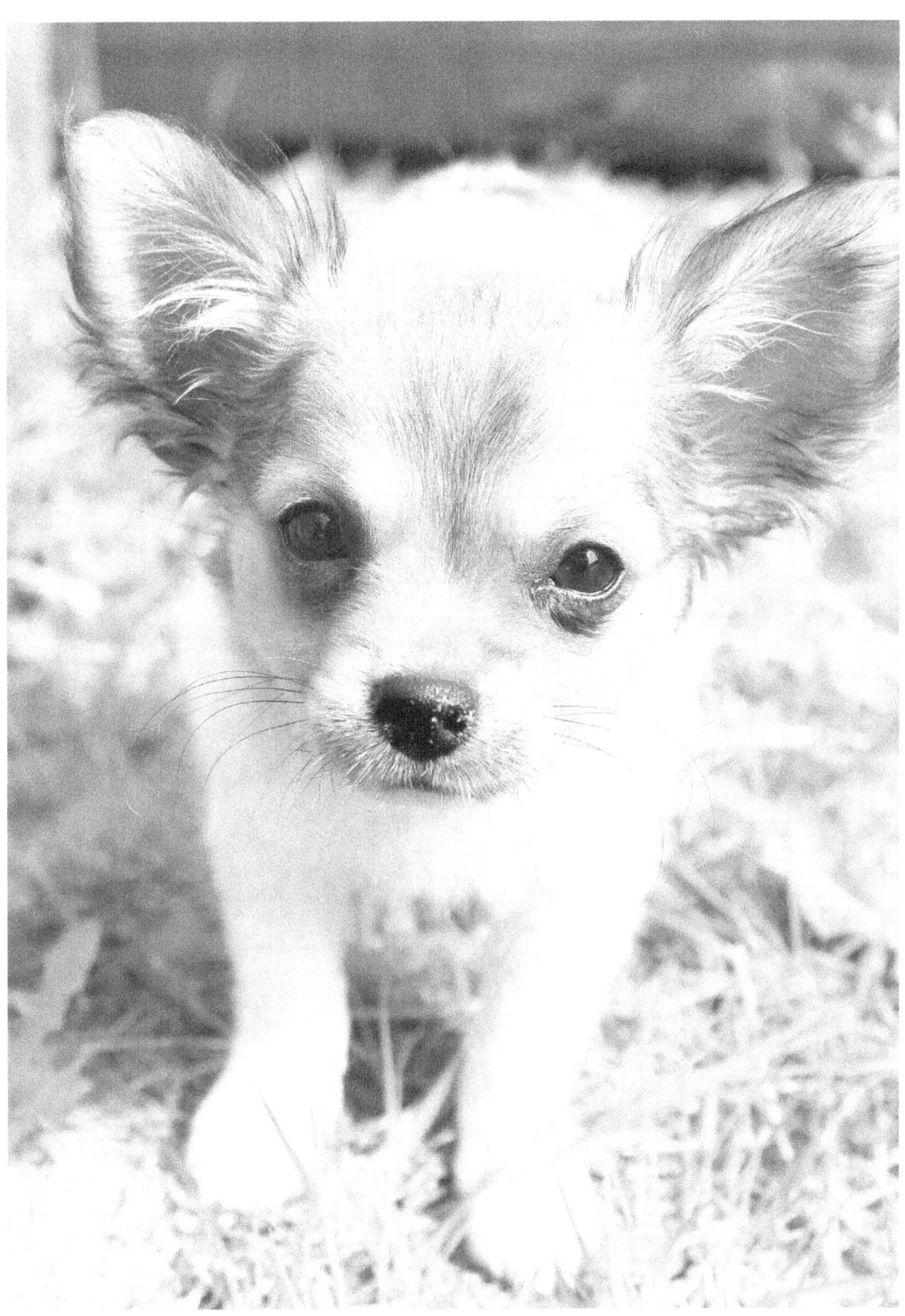

"It is amazing how much love and laughter puppies bring into our lives and even how much closer we become with each other because of them."
~ Josh Grogan

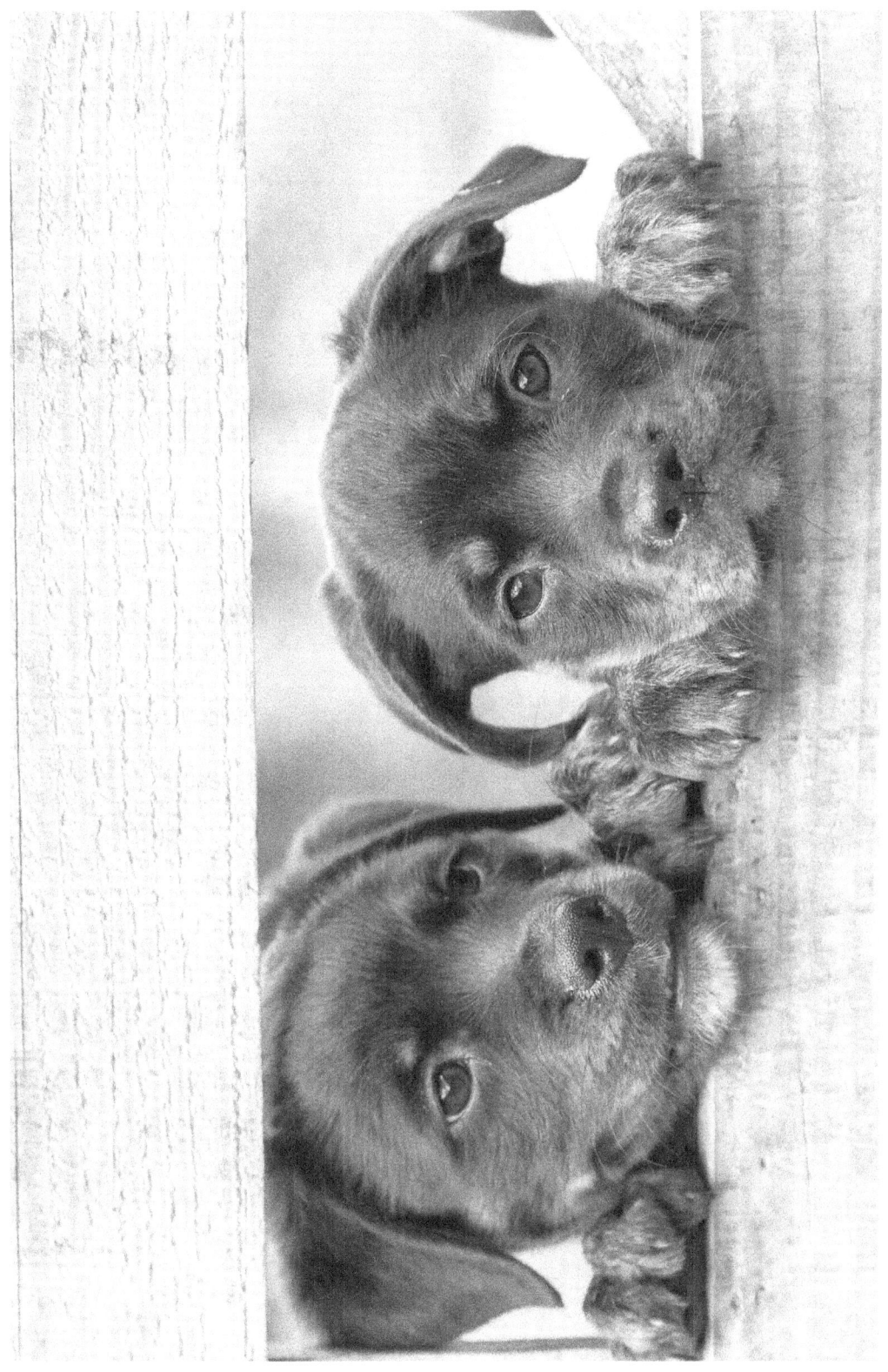

"A puppy gives us their absolute all. We are the center of their universe. We are the focus of their love and faith and trust. They serve us in return for scraps. It is without a doubt the best deal man has ever made."
~ Roger A. Caras

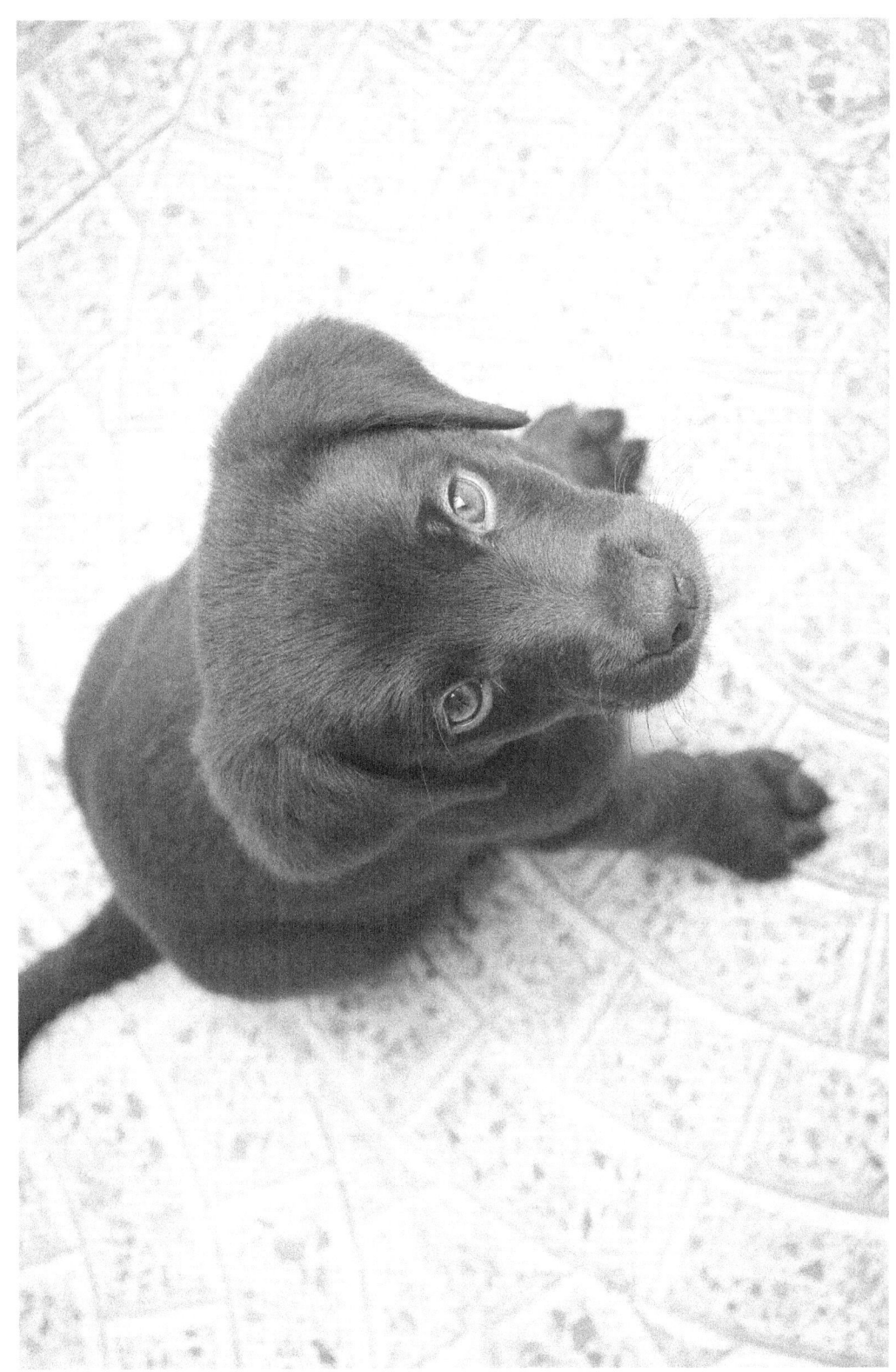

"I have found that when you are deeply troubled, there are things you get from the silent devoted companionship of a puppy that you can get from no other source."
~ Doris Day

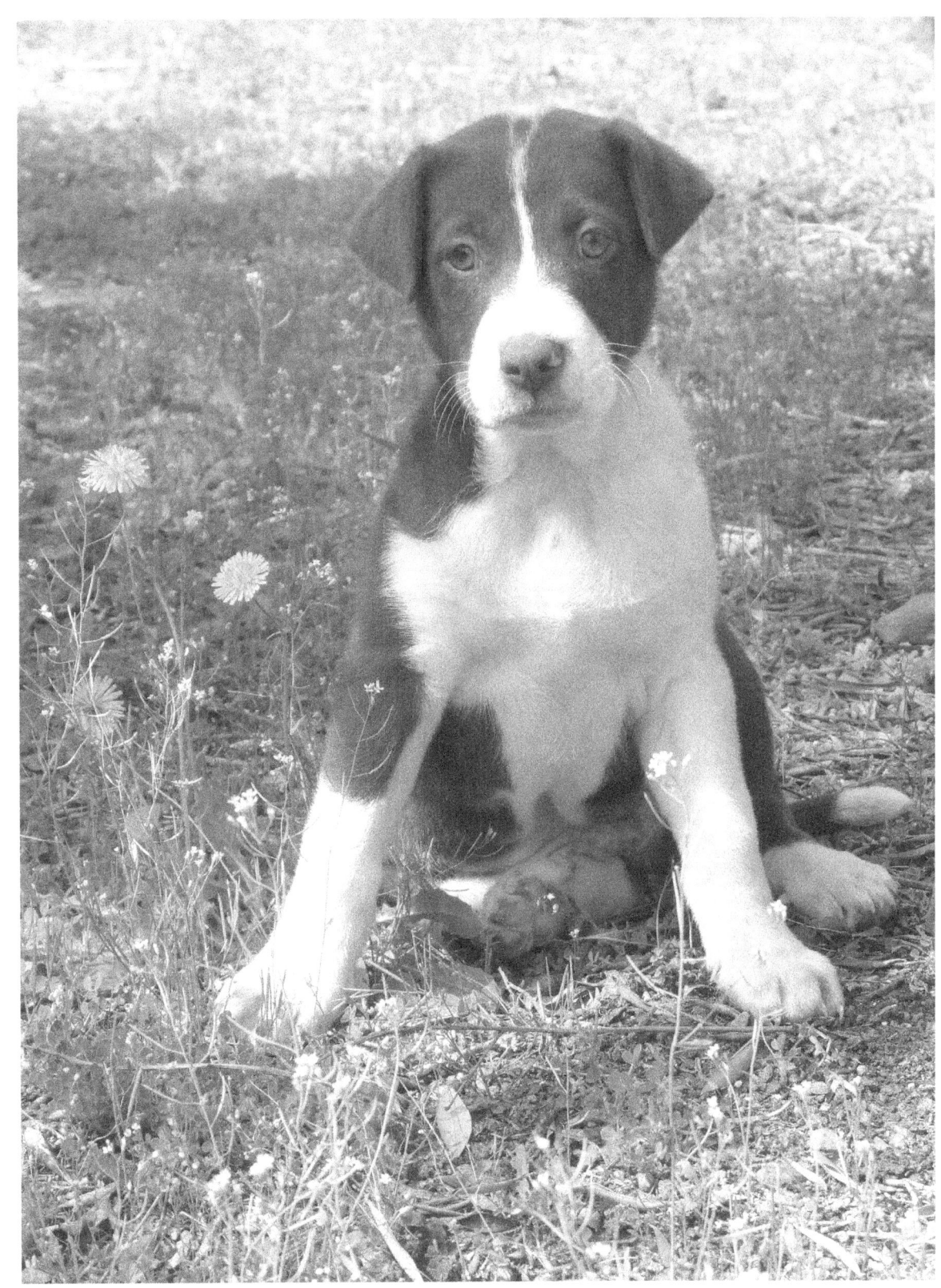

"I think puppies are the most amazing creatures; they give unconditional love. For me, they are the role model for being alive."
~ *Gilda Radner*

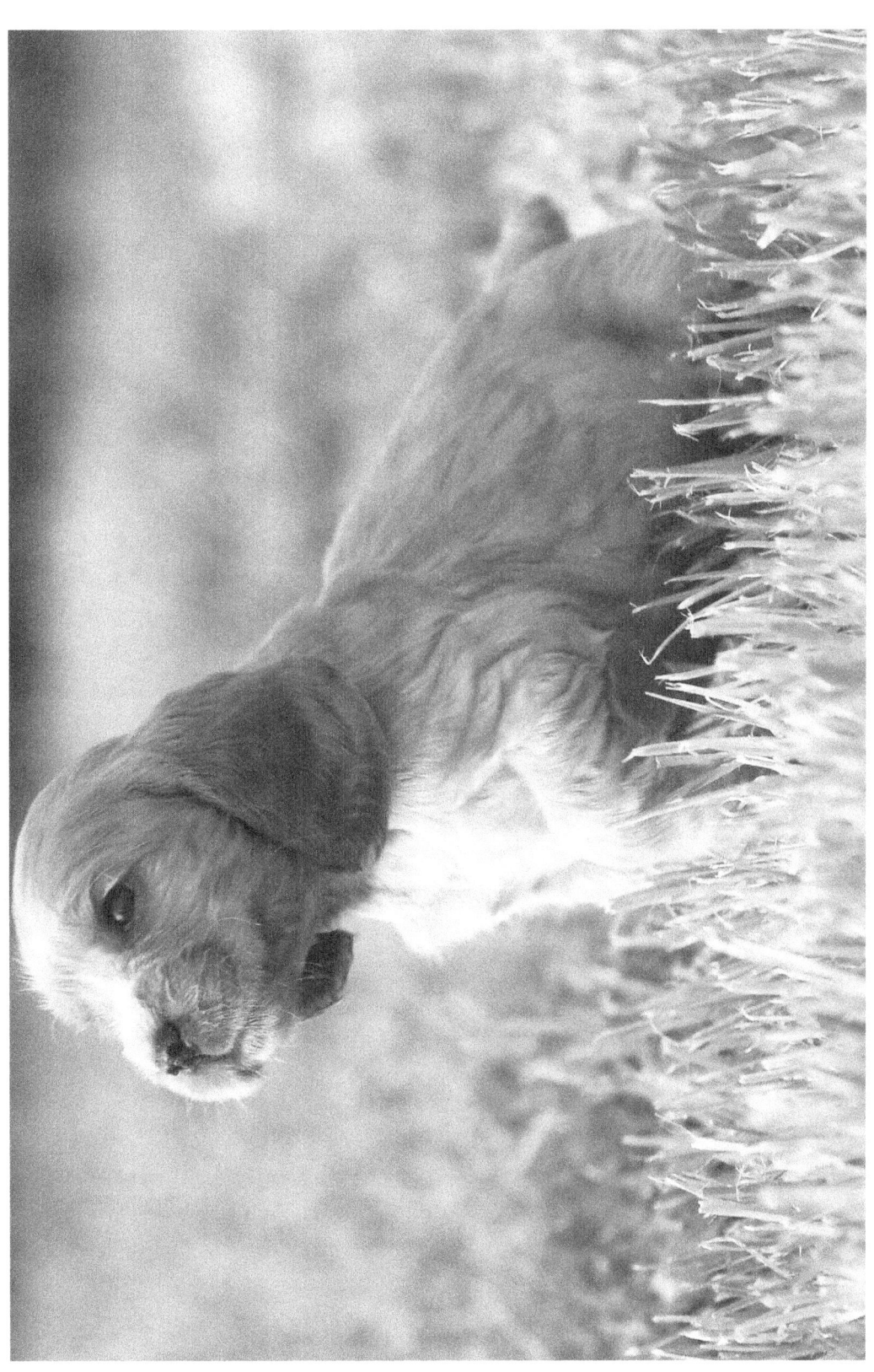

"Why does watching a puppy be a puppy fill one with happiness?"
~ Jonathan Safran Foer

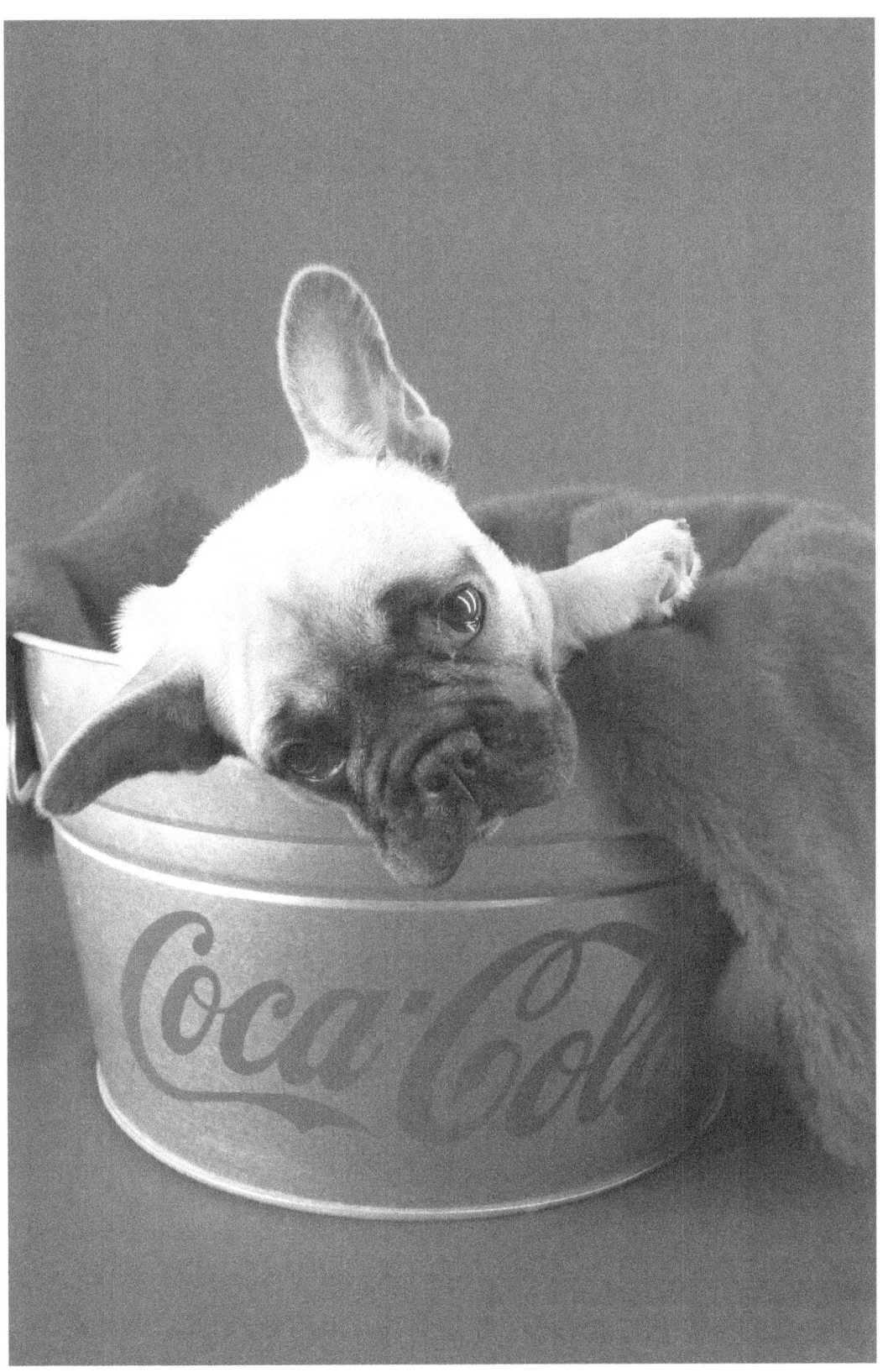

"The world would be a nicer place if everyone had the ability to love as unconditionally as a puppy."
~ M.K. Clinton

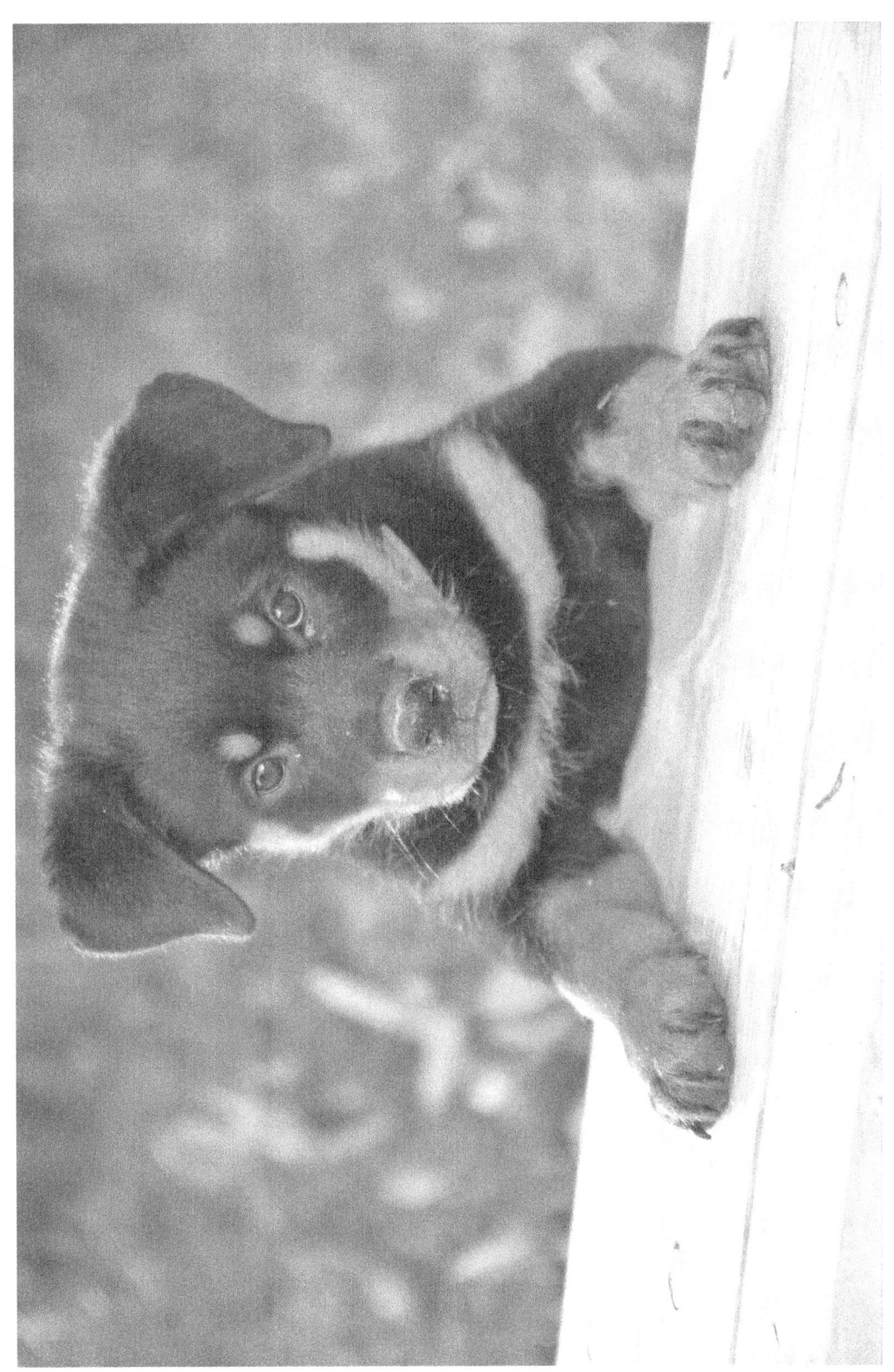

www.ingramcontent.com/pod-product-compliance
Lightning Source LLC
Chambersburg PA
CBHW062158220526
45470CB00009B/2857